Editor
Eric Migliaccio

Managing Editor
Ina Massler Levin, M.A.

Editor-in-Chief
Sharon Coan, M.S. Ed.

Illustrator
Bruce Hedges

Cover Artist
Janet Chadwick

Art Coordinator
Kevin Barnes

Art Director
CJae Froshay

Imaging
Rosa C. See

Product Manager
Phil Garcia

Publisher
Mary D. Smith, M.S. Ed.

GRADE 4

Author

Jeanne King

Teacher Created Resources, Inc.
6421 Industry Way
Westminster, CA 92683
www.teachercreated.com
ISBN: 978-0-7439-3363-6
©2003 Teacher Created Resources, Inc.
Reprinted, 2008
Made in U.S.A.

Table of Contents

Introduction

The old adage "practice makes perfect" can really hold true for your child and his or her education. The more practice and exposure your child has with concepts being taught in school, the more success he or she is likely to find. For many parents, knowing how to help their children may be frustrating because the resources may not be readily available.

As a parent it is also difficult to know where to focus your efforts so that the extra practice your child receives at home supports what he or she is learning in school.

Practice Makes Perfect: Vocabulary is designed to help practice word skills that are taught in the classroom. Vocabulary skills that are appropriate for fourth grade are presented in this book. Most of the words that appear in this book are standard vocabulary, but some special and unusual words are also included.

The following standards or objectives will be met or reinforced by completing the practice pages in this book. These standards and objectives are similar to the ones required by your state and school district. Fourth-grade students should be able to do the following:

- Use a dictionary to define vocabulary words
- Identify word meanings in context
- Use a thesaurus to identify synonyms and antonyms
- Identify and use homonyms, synonyms, and antonyms
- Identify root words, prefixes, and suffixes
- Change singular words into plurals
- Identify and use unusual plural words
- Develop everyday vocabulary
- Develop an on-going interest in learning and using new words.

Several exercises are provided for the student to practice each skill. There is also a section of word play to generate interest and prompt new learning. It is up to the adult to determine which pages are appropriate for his or her student.

An assessment unit at the end of the book reviews all of the concepts covered throughout the book. This assessment is provided in a standardized-test format to allow students to practice their knowledge as well as their test-taking skills.

How to Make the Most of This Book

Here are some useful ideas for making the most of this book:

- Set aside a specific place in your home to work on this book. Keep it neat and tidy, with the necessary materials on hand.
- Set up a certain time of day to work on these practice pages to establish consistency.
- Keep all practice sessions with your child positive and constructive. If your child becomes frustrated or tense set the book aside and look for another time to practice.
- Review the work your child has done.
- Pay attention to the areas in which your child has the most difficulty. Provide extra guidance and exercises in those areas.
- Look for ways to make real-life application to the skills being reinforced. Play vocabulary games with your child.

Learning New Words

How do you learn new words? You may ask an adult the meaning of a word. You may make a wild guess. But do you know other ways of learning new words? Here are some ideas.

I. You can learn a new word in a sentence.

For example:

The Earth makes an **orbit**, or "circle," around the sun every year.

The word *orbit* means "circle." Both words in the sentence help you understand the meaning of orbit. If you read a sentence with a new word, see if there is a word you know that can help you.

II. You can use clues in the sentence to help you make a good guess.

For example:

My grandmother told me my family's **ancestors** came from Africa.

The sentence tells you the speaker is talking about people in his family. The verb *came* tells you it already happened, so *ancestors* are probably people in his family from a long time ago.

III. You can break the word into its word parts: root word, prefix and/or suffix.

For example:

We had an **unusually** good day today.

Un is the prefix in this word; one of many prefixes that means "not." *Usual* means "normal," and *ly* is a suffix that turns an adjective into an adverb (a word that describes the verb, adjective or another adverb). So the word *unusually* means "not normally."

IV. You can use a dictionary to define the word.

A *dictionary* is a terrific tool. It tells you the meaning of a word. Dictionaries often have examples that tell you how a word is used.

V. You can use a thesaurus to find words you know that have about the same meaning.

A *thesaurus* is like a dictionary in that all the words are in alphabetical order. But a thesaurus will give you *synonyms*—words that mean the same as the word. A thesaurus may even have a section for *antonyms*—words that mean the opposite of the word.

Alphabetizing

To the First and Second Letter

One of the best ways to learn new words is to use the dictionary. The dictionary tells you the meaning or meanings of a word. Words in a dictionary are placed in alphabetical order. List the words below in alphabetical order. Alphabetize to the first letter. If some words have the same first letter, you must go to the second letter to see which comes first. Next, use your dictionary to find a definition for the word.

atmosphere	tropics	erosion	microscope
irrigate	mesa	tune	energy
crust	barter	corral	incisor
evaporate	friction	adaptation	foreign

Order	Definition
1. _____	_____
2. _____	_____
3. _____	_____
4. _____	_____
5. _____	_____
6. _____	_____
7. _____	_____
8. _____	_____
9. _____	_____
10. _____	_____
11. _____	_____
12. _____	_____
13. _____	_____
14. _____	_____
15. _____	_____
16. _____	_____

Alphabetizing *(cont.)*

To the Third and Fourth Letter

List the words below in alphabetical order. You will need to look at the third letter of each word. For example, *sea* and *servant* both begin with *se*, so you will need to look at the third letters *a* and *r*. *A* comes before *R* alphabetically: therefore, *sea* is placed before *servant* in alphabetical order.

inventor	industrial	inning	solar	solid
intense	independent	social	soil	southern
information	instrument	sod	solution	sore

Order	Definition

1. _____ _____
2. _____ _____
3. _____ _____
4. _____ _____
5. _____ _____
6. _____ _____
7. _____ _____
8. _____ _____
9. _____ _____
10. _____ _____
11. _____ _____
12. _____ _____
13. _____ _____
14. _____ _____
15. _____ _____

6

Using Guide Words

To look up words in the dictionary, you need to know about guide words. *Guide words* are the two words you find at the top of each dictionary page. The word on the top left tells you the first word on the page and the word on the right tells you the last word found on the page.

Put a checkmark (✓) next to the words you would find on each of these dictionary pages.

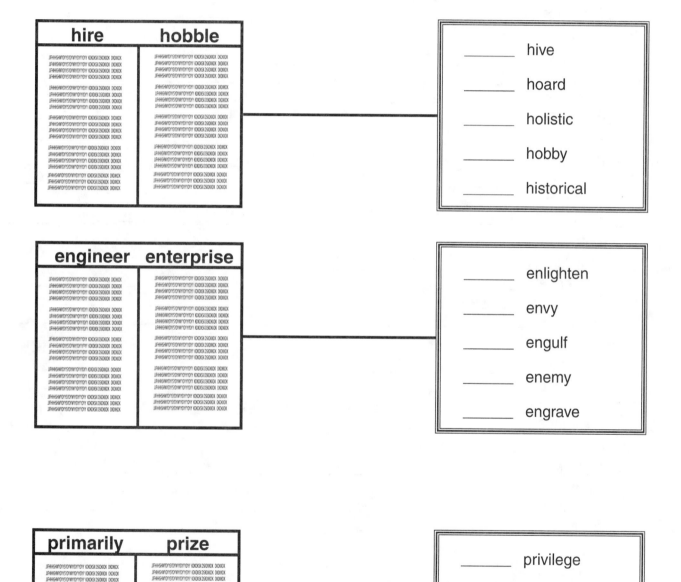

hire   **hobble**

_____ hive

_____ hoard

_____ holistic

_____ hobby

_____ historical

engineer   **enterprise**

_____ enlighten

_____ envy

_____ engulf

_____ enemy

_____ engrave

primarily   **prize**

_____ privilege

_____ pride

_____ prism

_____ prim

_____ price

Finding Definitions

Each of the words below has two or more definitions. Use a dictionary to find two meanings of each word. After each definition, write a sentence that uses the word in the same way.

1. **beam**
   Definition #1: _____
   Sentence:_____
   Definition #2: _____
   Sentence:_____

2. **check**
   Definition #1: _____
   Sentence:_____
   Definition #2: _____
   Sentence:_____

3. **date**
   Definition #1: _____
   Sentence:_____
   Definition #2: _____
   Sentence:_____

4. **habit**
   Definition #1: _____
   Sentence:_____
   Definition #2: _____
   Sentence:_____

5. **nurse**
   Definition #1: _____
   Sentence:_____
   Definition #2: _____
   Sentence:_____

6. **pad**
   Definition #1: _____
   Sentence:_____
   Definition #2: _____
   Sentence:_____

7. **range**
   Definition #1: _____
   Sentence:_____
   Definition #2: _____
   Sentence:_____

8. **scale**
   Definition #1: _____
   Sentence:_____
   Definition #2: _____
   Sentence:_____

8

Homophone Hunt

Homophones are words that sound the same but are spelled differently and have different meanings. Above each sentence are two homophones. Choose the one that is needed to make the sentence correct. Write your answer in the blank space. The first one has been done for you.

1. **bear** or **bare**

   After the leaves fell, the tree looked _____bare_____ .

2. **burro** or **burrow**

   The rabbit dove into its _____ quickly.

3. **creak** or **creek**

   The door made a loud _____ as it opened.

4. **doe** or **dough**

   The _____ wandered into the meadow with the other deer.

5. **hire** or **higher**

   The store owner said he would _____ the boy to make deliveries.

6. **knot** or **not**

   She tied a _____ around the tree to hold the rope in place.

7. **maid** or **made**

   The hotel had a _____ come in every day to make the beds.

8. **mane** or **main**

   She braided the horse's _____ before the parade.

9. **peace** or **piece**

   A feeling of _____ settled over the valley at night.

10. **pare** or **pear**

    The _____ tasted sweet.

11. **pain** or **pane**

    The ball crashed right through the window _____.

12. **soar** or **sore**

    They watched the eagle _____ through the air.

13. **sum** or **some**

    The _____ of 2 + 2 is 4.

14. **tale** or **tail**

    The teacher read a _____ about a tortoise and a hare.

15. **tide** or **tied**

    Once each day, the _____ covers the sand with water.

Heed Those Homonyms

Homonyms are words that are spelled and pronounced the same but may be used for different meanings. For example "a lock of hair" and "put the lock on the garage door." The word *lock* is used to mean two entirely different things. Read the sentences below. Focus on the underlined word in the first sentence. Bubble in the sentence below it that uses the word in the same way.

1. The doctor put a <u>cast</u> on his broken leg.
   - ⓐ After the play, the cast went to dinner.
   - ⓑ She wore her cast for six weeks.

2. Carrie looked at the plant <u>cells</u> under the microscope.
   - ⓐ People are made up of many cells.
   - ⓑ The prisoners were locked in their cells.

3. She put <u>jam</u> on her toast.
   - ⓐ His old typewriter had a paper jam.
   - ⓑ The farmers made jam from the strawberries.

4. She wove the tapestry on the <u>loom</u>.
   - ⓐ We watched the moon loom overhead.
   - ⓑ The lifted the cloth from the loom.

5. He made a <u>mold</u> of the dinosaur footprint.
   - ⓐ The leftovers were covered in mold.
   - ⓑ He poured the gelatin into its mold.

6. "Let's go <u>pitch</u> horseshoes in the park," said Jason.
   - ⓐ The mayor will pitch the first baseball of the season.
   - ⓑ We wanted to pitch the tent before nightfall.

7. The <u>pupils</u> at Glenkirk Elementary read 1,000 books in one month.
   - ⓐ The doctor flashed the light into her pupils.
   - ⓑ Fourteen pupils were honored at the assembly.

8. The crowd in the street made quite a <u>racket</u>.
   - ⓐ The racket from the house next door kept him awake.
   - ⓑ She got a new tennis racket for her birthday.

9. The <u>scale</u> said he weighed eighty pounds.
   - ⓐ The scale of a fish is different from the scale of a lizard.
   - ⓑ The nurse's scale was broken.

10. The <u>seal</u> pup barked for her mother.
    - ⓐ The president placed his official seal on the letter.
    - ⓑ The seal swam into the harbor looking for food.

Antonyms: Opposites Attract

Antonyms are words that mean the opposite of each other. For example: *good* and *bad*, *quiet* and *noisy*.

Look at the words in column 1. Find the antonym for each word in column 2. Write the letter of the antonym in column 2 next to its match in column 1. The first one has been done for you.

Column 1	Column 2
F 1. accept	A. lose
____ 2. bury	B. begin
____ 3. crooked	C. modesty
____ 4. disgust	D. approval
____ 5. familiar	E. strange
____ 6. gloomy	F. refuse
____ 7. hungry	G. straight
____ 8. locate	H. bright
____ 9. mysterious	I. unearth
____ 10. nonsense	J. untrustworthy
____ 11. obey	K. obvious
____ 12. pride	L. full
____ 13. quit	M. wisdom
____ 14. responsible	N. fat
____ 15. slender	O. ignore

Synonyms Are Similar

Synonyms are words that mean the same, or about the same, as another word. To find a synonym we use the *thesaurus*. Using synonyms in your writing helps keep writing fresh and helps us to avoid overusing words. Here is an example of a sentence that could use a few synonyms: *The good boy ate a very good lunch and said, "That was good."*

Use your thesaurus to find a synonym for each of the following words.

1. ache_____

2. argue_____

3. bulge_____

4. check_____

5. earnest_____

6. flutter_____

7. hesitate_____

8. jealous_____

9. locate_____

10. murmur_____

11. object_____

12. perform_____

13. prance_____

14. scamper_____

15. tilt_____

Now pick two of the synonyms from above and use them in a sentence. _____

_____

_____

Pick two more and use them in another sentence._____

_____

_____

Antonyms, Synonyms, or Homophones?

Decide whether the following pairs of words are antonyms, synonyms, or homophones. Check the box in the appropriate column. The first one has been done for you.

Pairs of Words	Antonym	Synonym	Homophone
1. maximum & minimum	✔	❏	❏
2. recall & remember	❏	❏	❏
3. allow & forbid	❏	❏	❏
4. chili & chilly	❏	❏	❏
5. often & frequently	❏	❏	❏
6. coarse & course	❏	❏	❏
7. birth & berth	❏	❏	❏
8. honest & sincere	❏	❏	❏
9. appear & vanish	❏	❏	❏
10. liberty & freedom	❏	❏	❏
11. gate & gait	❏	❏	❏
12. bright & dull	❏	❏	❏
13. easy & simple	❏	❏	❏
14. foreword & forward	❏	❏	❏
15. guessed & guest	❏	❏	❏
16. common & rare	❏	❏	❏
17. clear & plain	❏	❏	❏
18. herd & heard	❏	❏	❏
19. aid & assist	❏	❏	❏
20. defeat & victory	❏	❏	❏

Dividing Words by Syllables

Dividing words can be a tricky business, but if you know the four rules outlined here and on the pages that follow, it will become a snap. Read each rule carefully and apply your knowledge to the words below.

Rule #1

When a word has a double consonant, the word is divided between the two consonants.

Example: bub´-ble

Divide each word below into syllables, and place a stressed syllable mark (´) on the syllable you think is stressed. Use a dictionary to check your answers.

1. borrow _____

2. attic _____

3. banner _____

4. blizzard _____

5. effect _____

6. flutter _____

7. hobby _____

8. lettuce _____

9. mitten _____

10. stallion _____

11. soccer _____

12. pattern _____

13. stubborn _____

14. puzzle _____

15. ladder _____

16. falling _____

17. butter _____

Dividing Words by Syllables *(cont.)*

> ## Rule #2
> When a word ends in a consonant plus "le," the word is divided before the consonant.
> **Example:** pur´-ple

Divide each of the words below into syllables and place a stressed syllable mark (´) on the syllable you think is stressed. Again, use a dictionary to check your answers.

1. able _____

2. battle _____

3. castle _____

4. couple _____

5. grumble _____

6. jingle _____

7. mumble _____

8. paddle _____

9. stumble _____

10. tangle _____

11. table _____

12. noble _____

13. single _____

14. double _____

15. triple _____

16. noodle _____

17. turtle _____

Dividing Words by Syllables *(cont.)*

Rule #3

When the first vowel in a word has the short vowel sound the word is divided after the next consonant.

Example: lum´-ber

Divide each of the words below into syllables and place the stressed syllable mark on the syllable you think is stressed. Use a dictionary to check your answers.

1. artist _____

2. astound _____

3. bamboo _____

4. cargo _____

5. disease _____

6. explore _____

7. mixture _____

8. suspect _____

9. winter _____

10. vanish _____

11. message _____

12. listen _____

13. ponder _____

14. answer _____

15. stumble _____

16. ugly _____

17. trumpet _____

Dividing Words by Syllables *(cont.)*

Rule #4

When the first vowel in a word has the long vowel sound the word is divided after that vowel.

Example: De-cem´-ber

Divide each of the words below into syllables and place the stressed syllable mark on the syllable you think is stressed. Use a dictionary to check your answers.

1. bicycle _____

2. binary _____

3. curious _____

4. degree _____

5. favorite _____

6. human _____

7. motion _____

8. polar _____

9. deserve _____

10. zero _____

11. paper _____

12. cable _____

13. November _____

14. joker _____

15. receive _____

16. cucumber _____

17. tiger _____

Test Your Skills

Write each word and use a hyphen to divide the words into syllables. Then write the number of the rule(s) on the line that follows the word.

> **Rule #1:** When a word has a double consonant, the word is divided between the two consonants.
>
> **Rule #2:** When a word ends in a consonant plus "le," the word is divided before the consonant.
>
> **Rule #3:** When the first vowel in a word has the short vowel sound, the word is divided after the next consonant.
>
> **Rule #4:** When the first vowel in a word has the long vowel sound, the word is divided after that vowel.

	Syllables	Rule(s) #
1. acorn	_____	_____
2. attention	_____	_____
3. cobbler	_____	_____
4. December	_____	_____
5. corral	_____	_____
6. beetle	_____	_____
7. bottle	_____	_____
8. dandy	_____	_____
9. blubber	_____	_____
10. October	_____	_____
11. minstrel	_____	_____
12. stolen	_____	_____
13. stable	_____	_____
14. vanish	_____	_____
15. tropical	_____	_____

18

Rules for Plurals

Make a singular noun plural by adding *s*.

A noun is a person, place, or thing. When a noun is just one person, place, or thing, we say it is *singular*. For example, in the sentence "The girl walked away," the noun *girl* is singular. When the noun is talking about more than one person, place, or thing, we say the noun is *plural*. In the sentence "The girls walked away," the noun *girls* is plural. By adding *s* to the noun, we show we are speaking about more than one girl.

Directions: Add *s* to the following words to show the plural form of the noun.

Singular	Plural
1. car	_____
2. desk	_____
3. house	_____
4. tree	_____
5. boy	_____

We can't just add an *s* to every noun to make it plural, though. For nouns ending in *ch*, *s*, *sh*, *ss*, *x*, or *z*, we must add *es* to form the plural.

Add *es* to the following nouns to change them from singular to plural.

Singular	Plural
6. box	_____
7. church	_____
8. dish	_____
9. dress	_____
10. quartz	_____
11. sketch	_____
12. lens	_____
13. tax	_____
14. business	_____
15. glass	_____

What About Y?

Usually, if the final y in a word follows a vowel, as in boy, add s to form the plural. If the final *y* follows a consonant, change the y to *i* and add *es*. Remember, drop the *y* and add *ies*.

Change the following singular nouns to plural nouns.

Singular   **Plural**

1. baby   _____

2. donkey   _____

3. guy   _____

4. country   _____

5. copy   _____

6. lady   _____

7. day   _____

8. berry   _____

9. valley   _____

10. policy   _____

11. attorney   _____

12. delay   _____

13. century   _____

14. fly   _____

15. bunny   _____

Now, pick at least two of the plurals you've just written and use them in a sentence.

_____

_____

_____

What Is Normal, Anyway?

Many nouns in English do not follow the plural rules. They are called *irregular nouns* (not regular). The plurals of the following words do not fit the normal rules for plurals. Use your dictionary to find the plural of each word.

Singular   **Plural**

1. child   _____

2. foot   _____

3. goose   _____

4. man   _____

5. mouse   _____

6. ox   _____

7. tooth   _____

8. woman   _____

9. deer   _____

10. fish   _____

11. moose   _____

12. sheep   _____

Now, pick at least two of the plurals you've just written and use them in a sentence.

_____

_____

_____

Getting to the Root of Prefixes

Most large words can be broken into smaller units of meaning.

➢ Prefixes

Parts of words called *prefixes* are fixed to the beginning of the root word to change its meaning. Each prefix has its own meaning. The prefixes *il*, *un*, *non*, *ir*, *in*, and *im* all mean *not*.

➢ Root Words

The *root word* is the main part of the word, and the root word is a whole word that can stand alone, unlike prefixes and suffixes. If you know the meaning of the prefix and the root word, you can figure out the word meaning.

Separate the words in the spaces provided to figure out the word meaning. The first one is done for you.

	Prefix		Root Word		Meaning
1. illegal =	il		legal		not legal
2. illogical =	_____	+	_____	=	_____
3. impatient =	_____	+	_____	=	_____
4. inactive =	_____	+	_____	=	_____
5. inattentive =	_____	+	_____	=	_____
6. incomplete =	_____	+	_____	=	_____
7. indirect =	_____	+	_____	=	_____
8. inhuman =	_____	+	_____	=	_____
9. irregular =	_____	+	_____	=	_____
10. nonsense =	_____	+	_____	=	_____
11. nonstop =	_____	+	_____	=	_____
12. unpleasant =	_____	+	_____	=	_____
13. unnatural =	_____	+	_____	=	_____
14. unnecessary =	_____	+	_____	=	_____

Getting To the Root of Prefixes *(cont.)*

The dictionary lists prefixes as entries. These parts of words, when added to a root word, change the word's meaning. Use your dictionary to find the meaning of each prefix below. Next, match its meaning to the prefix.

	Prefixes		**Meanings**
_____	1. un-	A.	twice *or* two
_____	2. re-	B.	again
_____	3. pre-	C.	not
_____	4. mis-	D.	bad, wrongly, *or* badly
_____	5. in-, im-	E.	three
_____	6. bi-	F.	before
_____	7. tri-	G.	not *or* a lack of

Now, add the prefixes to a root word below to create a new word. Choose from the root words in the box. Use each root word only once. Check your word in the dictionary.

cycle	annual	produce	caution
angle	tangle	lead	complete

Prefix	**Root Word**		**New Word**
8. un +	_____	=	_____
9. re +	_____	=	_____
10. pre +	_____	=	_____
11. mis +	_____	=	_____
12. in +	_____	=	_____
13. bi +	_____	=	_____
14. tri +	_____	=	_____

Suffering Suffixes

Just as prefixes each have their own meanings, so do suffixes. Break each of the words below into its root word and suffix. You see how easy it is to figure out its meaning.

- *-able* and *-ible* mean "capable of" or "able to do" as in *manageable* or *workable*

- *-an* means "belonging to" as in *African* or *American*

- *-est* means "most" as in *closest* or *slowest*

- *-ful* means "full of" as in *colorful* or *playful*

- *-ish* means "of" or "like" as in *freakish* or *brutish*

- *-less* means "without" as in *homeless* or *senseless*

- *-or* means "a performer of action" as in *actor* or *sailor*

Add a suffix to the end of each root word from above to change its meaning. Check your answer in your dictionary. Write the definition of the new word in the space provided.

1. act _____

   Definition:_____

2. child _____

   Definition:_____

3. thank _____

   Definition:_____

4. collect _____

   Definition:_____

5. mean _____

   Definition:_____

6. change _____

   Definition:_____

7. Haiti _____

   Definition:_____

Idioms

An *idiom* is a commonly used expression or phrase that means something entirely different from its literal meaning (what it appears to mean). For example, if something is "a piece of cake" it means it is easy.

Below are some commonly used idioms. Use them to complete the activities on pages 26 and 27.

Idiom	Meaning
"Cat got your tongue?"	"Is there a reason you're not speaking?"
"hit the nail on the head"	to be exactly correct or come to the right conclusion
"throw in the towel"	to give up, or to quit
"by the skin of your teeth"	just barely, or a really close call
"fly off the handle"	to lose your temper quickly
"once in a blue moon"	almost never, very seldom
"one-track mind"	always thinking about only one thing
"nutty as a fruitcake"	crazy, or extremely strange
"I'm all ears"	"I'm eager to listen."

Write a short paragraph using at least three of the idioms listed above.

_____

_____

_____

_____

_____

_____

_____

_____

_____

Pictionary of Idioms

Look at the idioms below. Draw a picture of what the phrase would look like if we took the phrase or expression literally.

Example: "I'm all ears."

1. "You hit the nail on the head."	2. "I think I'll throw in the towel."
3. "She's as nutty as a fruitcake."	4. "What's the matter? Cat got your tongue?"

 © Teacher Created Resources, Inc.

Idioms Crossword Puzzle

Read the clues listed below the puzzle. In the each one, there is one word that makes the sentence wrong. In the puzzle, write the word that correctly completes the idiom.

Across

4. When you can't speak, someone might ask you, "What's the matter? Cat got your foot?"

5. When the boxer decided to quit, he said, "I'm going to throw in the glove."

6. His boss was always mad and ready to fly off the broom at any moment.

Down

1. Timmy always thinks about football. He has a one-track head.

2. His favorite team was terrible. They seemed to win only once in a red moon.

3. Crazy Steve was as crunchy as a fruitcake.

4. He barely won the race by the skin of his elbow.

7. After I guessed the correct answer, my uncle said, "You hit the hammer on the head."

8. My sister wanted to talk, and I told her, "I'm all eyes."

Parts of a Computer

Look at the picture below. It shows a computer station with all of the parts of the computer labeled. See page 29 for definitions of these computer parts.

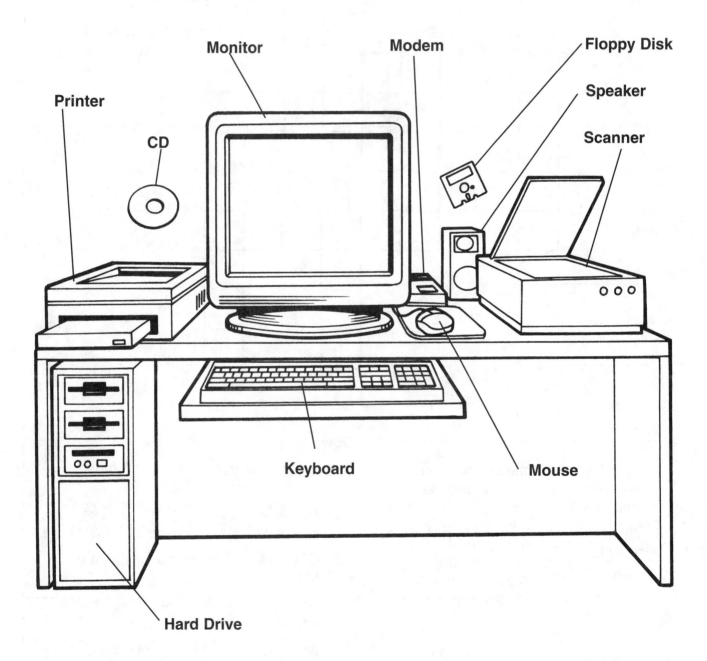

Parts of a Computer *(cont.)*

Computers seem to speak their own language. The basic vocabulary words you need to know to understand your computer are listed below. Cut out the boxes below to make a set of flash cards to help you prepare for the quiz on page 30.

— CD — A *CD* is a round circle or disk that holds information or music that your computer is able to read.	**— Floppy Disk —** A *floppy disk* is a small, thin piece of plastic used for storing information for or from your computer.
— Hard Drive — The *hard drive* is a machine that has a lot of memory to save your work and it can carry a CD and a floppy disk.	**— Keyboard —** The *keyboard* is a tool that is used for typing either on a computer or a typewriter.
— Modem — A *modem* is the part of the computer that connects to the phone lines so that you can go on the Internet.	**— Monitor —** The *monitor* is the screen on your computer that you look at when you are using the computer.
— Mouse — A *mouse* is a piece of plastic that has a ball on the bottom and two buttons on top. Clicking and moving the mouse allows you to move the cursor on your computer.	**— Printer —** A *printer* is a machine that puts words or pictures from the computer onto paper.
— Scanner — A *scanner* is a piece of equipment that copies pictures so that you can use them in your computer projects.	**— Speaker —** A *speaker* is the part of the computer that lets your hear the sounds from the programs.

Label the Computer

Use the word box to label the parts of the computer.

Word Box

- mouse
- modem
- keyboard
- scanner

- floppy disk
- monitor
- speaker

- hard drive
- CD
- printer

Words That Make the World Go Round

Many words that we use in social studies deal with maps of our neighborhoods, our cities, our states, our countries and our world. Using either your glossary in your social studies text or your dictionary, find the meanings of the following words.

Danger! Multiple Meanings Ahead!: Look only for the definitions that relate to maps and map skills. Good luck!

1. equator _____

2. geography _____

3. hemisphere _____

4. key _____

5. latitude _____

6. legend _____

7. longitude _____

8. meridians _____

9. polar _____

10. prime meridian _____

11. rural _____

12. scale _____

13. symbol _____

14. tropics _____

15. urban _____

Map Match

Now that you know what your social studies words mean, match the words in the Word Bank with their meanings on the map. The first one is done for you.

Word Bank

A. equator   C. tropics   E. key   G. scale

B. hemisphere   D. polar   F. prime meridian

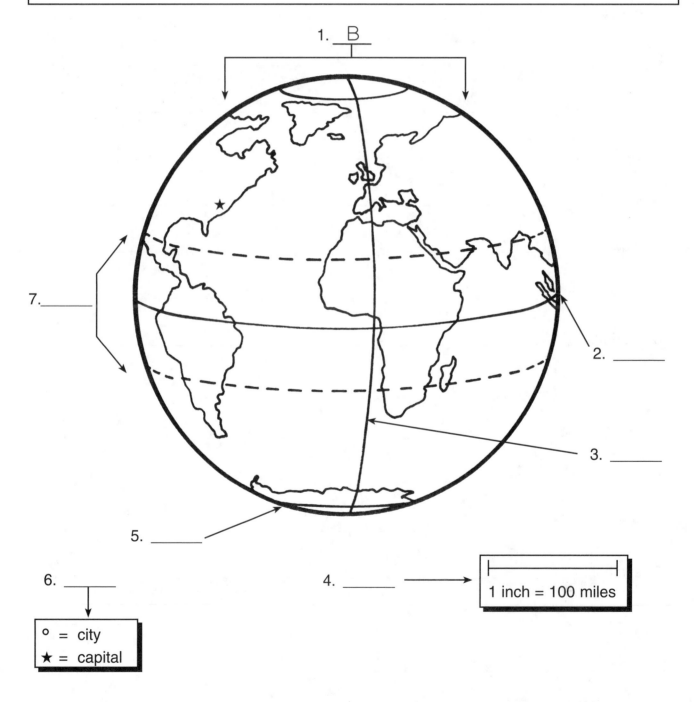

1. B

7. ____

2. ____

3. ____

5. ____

4. ____ 1 inch = 100 miles

6. ____

° = city
★ = capital

     32

Signs and Symbols

Mathematics consists of numbers and also words. However, there are also many symbols that represent words we need to know. Get to know the symbols and their meanings on the list below, and you will become a math whiz.

Symbol or Abbreviation	Meaning
lb.	means *pound*. Add an *s* to make it plural.
oz.	the abbreviated form of *ounce* or *ounces*
cm	means *centimeter*
m	for *meter*
in.	is the same as *inch* or *inches*
"	is also a way of saying *inch* or *inches*
ft.	means *foot* or *feet*
'	also means *foot* or *feet*
=	shows something is *equal* or *equivalent*
≠	means *not equal*
<	*less than* (example: 3 < 7)
>	*greater than* (example: 7 > 3)
#	stands for *number*

Now fill in the sentences below with the correct symbol or abbreviation.

1. My sister Jane weighs 63 _____.

2. I drank an 8- _____ glass of juice this morning.

3. The number 50 is _____ the number 49, but < the number 51.

4. In math class, we learned that 100 cm = 1 _____.

5. Did you know that 12 _____ = 1 _____?

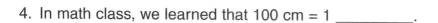

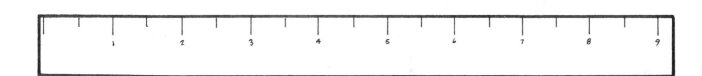

Do You Speak Math?

Math or mathematics has a language all its own. To do your math well in school, you need to understand this special language. Look at the words in Column 1. On the line provided, put the letter of its matching definition from Column 2. You will need to check your dictionary.

Column 1

_____ 1. area

_____ 2. congruent

_____ 3. difference

_____ 4. equation

_____ 5. parallel

_____ 6. perimeter

_____ 7. perpendicular

_____ 8. product

_____ 9. quotient

_____ 10. sum

Column 2

A. a line that is at right angles to another line

B. the answer to a subtraction problem

C. lines that run side by side that never cross and never meet

D. the answer to an addition problem

E. equal in shape or size

F. the distance around the edge of a shape (side + side + side + side)

G. a number sentence or statement

H. the answer to a multiplication problem

I. the amount of surface within a given boundary. It is measured in square units.

J. the answer to a division problem

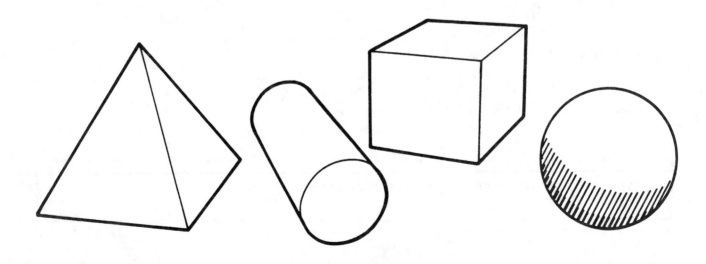

Do You Speak Math? *(cont.)*

We do not really know a language until we learn to use it well. See if you can give some examples of your math language.

1. Write a number sentence and underline the **sum**.

   _____

2. Write a number sentence and circle the **product**.

   _____

3. Write a number sentence and draw a box around the **quotient**.

   _____

4. Write a number sentence and put a triangle around the **difference**.

   _____

5. Write the formula you would use to show the **perimeter of a triangle**.

   _____

6. What is the **area** of the following rectangle?

   _____

7. Which of the following items is **congruent** to this figure?

   a.   b.   c.   d.

8. Draw two **parallel lines**.

   _____

9. Draw two **perpendicular lines**.

   _____

10. Write an **equation** using only the following three numbers: 6, 3, and 9.

   _____

Science Words

Find the words that fit each definition. Use the word bank and your dictionary to solve the riddle.

Word Bank

analyze	cite	experiment	observe
chart	data	hypothesis	variable

Word   **Clue**

__ __ ○ __ __ __ __ __ __   a scientific test to find out something new
       1

__ __ __ __ __ __ ○ __   a prediction that can be tested
                      3

__ __ ○ __ __ __   to watch something carefully
       5

__ ○ __ __ __ __ __   to examine something carefully in order to
   6   understand it

○ __ __ __   information or facts
4

__ __ __ ○ __   to quote from a written work; to give
          8   credit to

○ __ __ __ __   a drawing that shows information in the
7   form of a table, graph, or picture

○ __ __ __ __ __ __ __   likely to change
2

Solve the Riddle: What does a scientist need in order to prove something is true?

__ __ __ __ __ __ __ __
1   2   3   4   5   6   7   8

Analogies

Analogies are comparisons. They show relationships between words. Complete each analogy below. An example has been done for you.

Example: Nephew is to uncle as niece is to aunt.

1. _____ is to wings as fish is to fins.

2. Tennis is to _____ as baseball is to bat.

3. Author is to story as poet is to _____.

4. Wide is to narrow as _____ is to short.

5. Lincoln is to _____ as Roosevelt is to Theodore.

6. _____ is to shell as pea is to pod.

7. Hard is to _____ as big is to small.

8. Dirt is to forest as _____ is to desert.

9. Frame is to picture as curtain is to _____.

10. Sing is to song as _____ is to book.

11. Braces are to _____ as contact lenses are to eyes.

12. _____ is to flake as rain is to drop.

13. Scissors is to _____ as pen is to write.

14. Hat is to head as _____ is to foot.

15. Fingers are to _____ as toes are to feet.

Palindromes

Palindromes are words, phrases, sentences, or numbers that read the same forward and backward. Write a palindrome that relates to each word or phrase below. An example has been done for you.

Example: small dog = pup

1. man's name _____

2. past tense of the verb do _____

3. relating to government or citizenship _____

4. 12 o'clock _____

5. woman in a convent _____

6. female sheep _____

7. a flower _____

8. little chick's noise _____

9. ancient king _____

10. Eskimo canoe _____

11. small child _____

12. woman's name _____

13. flat, even _____

14. trick or joke _____

15. songs sung alone _____

Palindromes Word Search

Palindromes are numbers, phrases, words, and sentences that read the same forward and backward. Examples are *mom* and *121*. See how many palindromes you can find in this puzzle.

```
S C O M L K B B U Y F M R E W E Q T F
L D P A A C O I D F N U N T R H N H U
E O I E C B Q A B J T M M O E A B T H
V T M Y E P D K P K N L T A O N H I O
E O O J X P M G M O R I Q D D N E A U
L O W T U W N I T R Q M Q H O A E T S
B T J P S R N U Y Z K B R S T H M V T
N A D D B D R R Z P L J O O U Q O J E
J Z S O Z I A S H V O H E L T R Z O O
D E E D M G D B A Q S P W O C O Z X T
X Y B O O M A G K A A L P S I K R A T
T E Q B M R R G W D G Z F R V G V B O
E A R K N L S L O I A L U P I K O O C
R E P A P E R U W D S N I O C M L T O
R K H Y O X P R M J N E N T E R K G G
E O J A F O I U X K P M B A C E B I S
T H A K D J N N X R G G E Z C A O T Q
S E E S U Y G D A W Z P B H A B D T W
W L S R D S S P J A V E S C P F N M G
```

Similes

A *simile* is a figure of speech in which two unlike things are compared using the words *like* or *as*.

Example: He moved as quick as a wink.

Use the word bank to complete the following common similes.

1. As fresh as a _____

2. As white as _____

3. As wise as an _____

4. As strong as an _____

5. As flat as a _____

6. As cold as _____

7. As hard as _____

8. As stubborn as a _____

9. As cute as a _____

10. As black as _____

11. As blind as a _____

12. As happy as a _____

13. As cool as a _____

14. As stiff as a _____

15. As pretty as a _____

16. As busy as a _____

17. As light as a _____

18. As good as _____

Word Bank

• snow	• feather	• pancake
• daisy	• button	• board
• ox	• coal	• bee
• gold	• nails	• ice
• owl	• bat	• lark
• mule	• cucumber	• picture

What's Your Etymology?

Words in English come from a variety of different cultures and countries. Read the *etymology,* or word history, for the following words.

- **Fun** stems from the word *fon,* which meant "to make a fool of."

- **Hibernate** comes from the Latin word *hibernus,* which means "wintry."

- The English word **pen** comes from the Latin word *penna,* which means "feather." People once wrote with quill pens made from bird feathers.

- The **porpoise**'s name comes from a French word that came from the Latin words *porcus,* which means "pig," and *piscis,* which means "fish." Early people thought the porpoise's nose looked like that of a pig.

- The **pupil** of the eye got its name from the Latin word *pupilla,* which means "tiny doll." The tiny reflection a person sees when he looks into another person's eyes gave this small part of the eye its name.

- The word **robot** got its name from the Czech word *robota,* which means "forced labor."

- **Skeleton** comes from the Greek expression *soma skeleton.* This phrase meant "dried-up body."

Many of the names of the days of the week credit their history to mythology.

- **Sunday** comes from the Roman phrase "sun's day."

- **Monday** is from Latin. It was originally "moon's day."

- **Tuesday** was named for *Tiw,* the English god of war.

- **Wednesday** was named after *Woden,* the Scandinavian god of agriculture.

- *Thor,* the Norse god of thunder, gave his name to **Thursday**.

- In pagan England, they worshipped many gods; but *Frigga* was the queen of the gods. The English named **Friday** after this queen.

- **Saturday** was named for *Saturn,* the Roman god of farming.

Unit Assessment

Read each question carefully. Mark the best answer. Fill in the bubble completely.

1. Which of these word lists are in alphabetical order?
   - (a) mud, most, mean
   - (b) food, feet, fate
   - (c) gaze, grow, green
   - (d) rage, rinse, rust

2. Which of these word lists are in alphabetical order?
   - (a) drain, drape, drip
   - (b) side, said, shield
   - (c) join, cake, jade
   - (d) heat, hare, hear

3. The guide words at the top of the dictionary page are *caught* and *dime*. Which of these words *would not* be on the page?
   - (a) cave
   - (b) disease
   - (c) diet
   - (d) deal

4. The guide words at the top are *gem* and *gesture*. Which of these words *would not* be found on the page?
   - (a) general
   - (b) germ
   - (c) gentle
   - (d) geyser

5. Which sentence uses the word *piece* correctly?
   - (a) There was a feeling of piece in the room.
   - (b) He broke a piece of bread in two.
   - (c) The president signed the piece treaty.
   - (d) She said she wanted some piece and quiet.

6. Which sentence uses the word *tale* correctly?
   - (a) We played "Pin the Tale on the Donkey."
   - (b) A rat has a long tale.
   - (c) We read *The Tale of Peter Rabbit*.
   - (d) The skunk had a white stripe on its tale.

7. Which word is a synonym for *locate*?
   - (a) lose
   - (b) show
   - (c) donate
   - (d) find

8. Which word is a synonym for *argument*?
   - (a) quarrel
   - (b) might
   - (c) peaceful
   - (d) thoughtfulness

9. Which word is a not a synonym for *flutter*?
   - (a) beat
   - (b) flap
   - (c) vibrate
   - (d) dance

Unit Assessment *(cont.)*

10. Which word is a synonym for *scamper*?
    - (a) run
    - (b) hamper
    - (c) crawl
    - (d) juggle

11. Which word is an antonym for *slender*?
    - (a) thin
    - (b) cold
    - (c) fat
    - (d) tiny

12. Which word is an antonym for *bad*?
    - (a) sad
    - (b) awful
    - (c) happy
    - (d) good

13. Which word is an antonym for *hungry*?
    - (a) empty
    - (b) full
    - (c) hollow
    - (d) starved

14. Which word is an antonym for *quit*?
    - (a) stop
    - (b) begin
    - (c) cease
    - (d) lit

For #15–19, choose the correct way to divide the following words.

15. bedding
    - (a) bed-ding
    - (b) bedd-ing
    - (c) be-dding
    - (d) b-edding

16. battle
    - (a) b-attle
    - (b) ba-ttle
    - (c) batt-le
    - (d) bat-tle

17. expense
    - (a) e-xpense
    - (b) exp-ense
    - (c) ex-pense
    - (d) expen-se

18. hotel
    - (a) h-otel
    - (b) ho-tel
    - (c) hot-el
    - (d) hote-l

19. ladle
    - (a) l-adle
    - (b) lad-le
    - (c) la-dle
    - (d) ladl-e

Unit Assessment *(cont.)*

20. Which of these plurals is misspelled?
    - (a) mooses
    - (b) trucks
    - (c) ladies
    - (d) sketches

21. Which of these plurals is misspelled?
    - (a) businesses
    - (b) delays
    - (c) centurys
    - (d) attorneys

22. Which of these plurals is misspelled?
    - (a) lynxes
    - (b) markes
    - (c) masks
    - (d) clocks

23. Which of these plurals is misspelled?
    - (a) wishes
    - (b) sheeps
    - (c) women
    - (d) deer

24. Which of these shows the meaning of the prefix *un-*?
    - (a) full
    - (b) again
    - (c) not
    - (d) before

25. Which of these shows the meaning of the prefix *re-*?
    - (a) not
    - (b) before
    - (c) again
    - (d) two

26. Which of these shows the meaning of the prefix *pre-*?
    - (a) again
    - (b) not
    - (c) two
    - (d) before

27. Which of these shows the meaning of the prefix *bi-*?
    - (a) again
    - (b) not
    - (c) three
    - (d) two

Unit Assessment *(cont.)*

28. Which of these meanings is the same as the suffix *-less*?
    - (a) most
    - (b) without
    - (c) having the ability
    - (d) full of

29. Which of these shows the meaning of the suffix *-ful*?
    - (a) full of
    - (b) without
    - (c) having the ability
    - (d) most

30. Which of these shows the meaning of the suffix *-est*?
    - (a) full of
    - (b) without
    - (c) most
    - (d) having the ability

31. Which of these shows the meaning of the suffix *-or*?
    - (a) the performer of
    - (b) without
    - (c) having the ability
    - (d) most

32. Which of these is an imaginary line that runs around the middle of the earth that divides the Northern hemisphere from the Southern?
    - (a) polar
    - (b) meridian
    - (c) latitude
    - (d) equator

33. Which of these is an imaginary line that runs around the Earth that divides the Eastern and Western hemispheres?
    - (a) longitude
    - (b) prime meridian
    - (c) equator
    - (d) tropics

34. Which of these is the symbol for *pound*?
    - (a) m.
    - (b) oz.
    - (c) lb.
    - (d) >

35. Which of these is the symbol for is *not equal to*?
    - (a) $\neq$
    - (b) <
    - (c) >
    - (d) #

36. Which of these is the answer to a division problem?
    - (a) quotient
    - (b) divisor
    - (c) congruent
    - (d) product

Answer Key

Page 5

Answers will vary

1. adaptation—the change a living thing goes through so it fits better in its environment
2. atmosphere—the mixture of gases that surrounds a planet; a mood or feeling
3. barter—to trade by exchanging food or other goods or services
4. corral—a fenced area that holds animals or to gather living things in an enclosed area
5. crust—the outer layer of bread, pastry, or Earth
6. energy—power from a source or the ability of something to do work
7. erosion—the gradual wearing away of a substance
8. evaporate—changing into a vapor or gas; to become less and then disappear
9. foreign—to do with or coming from another country; unnatural
10. friction—rubbing; a disagreement or anger
11. incisor—a cutting tooth at the front of the mouth
12. irrigate—to supply water to crops
13. mesa—a hill or mountain with steep sides and a flat top
14. microscope—an instrument that magnifies very small things
15. tropics—the extremely hot area of the earth near the equator
16. tune—a series of musical notes arranged in a pattern

Page 6

Answers will vary slightly

1. independent—free from the control of other people or things
2. industrial—to do with businesses and factories
3. information—facts and knowledge
4. inning—part of a baseball game in which each team gets to bat
5. instrument—an object you use to make music; a tool or other apparatus
6. intense—very strong
7. inventor—one who creates something
8. social—to do with people getting together
9. sod—the top layer of soil and the grass attached to it
10. soil—dirt or earth in which plants grow
11. solar—to do with the sun
12. solid—hard and firm; not hollow
13. solution—the answer to a problem; a mixture
14. sore—painful; angry
15. southern—in or toward the south

Page 7

1. hive, hoard, historical
2. enlighten, engulf, engrave
3. privilege, prism

Page 8

Sentences and definitions will vary. Two or more definitions are available on each word.

1. **beam**

   Definition #1: a ray or band of light

   Definition #2: a long, thick piece of wood, concrete, or metal

2. **check**

   Definition #1: a printed piece of paper on which someone writes to tell the bank to pay money from his or her account

   Definition #2: to look at something in order to make sure it is all right

3. **date**

   Definition #1: a certain particular day, month, or year

   Definition #2: an appointment

4. **habit**

   Definition #1: something done regularly

   Definition #2: clothing worn for a particular activity

5. **nurse**

   Definition #1: someone who looks after people who are sick

   Definition #2: to treat with care

6. **pad**

   Definition #1: to walk around softly

   Definition #2: sheets of paper fastened together

7. **range**

   Definition #1: to vary greatly

   Definition #2: an area of open land used for a special purpose

8. **scale**

   Definition #1: a piece of hard skin that covers a fish or reptile

   Definition #2: an instrument used for weighing things

Page 9

1. bare
2. burrow
3. creak
4. doe
5. hire
6. knot
7. maid
8. mane
9. peace
10. pear
11. pane
12. soar
13. sum
14. tale
15. tide

Page 10

1. b		6. a	
2. a		7. b	
3. b		8. a	
4. b		9. b	
5. b		10. b	

Page 11

1. F		9. K	
2. I		10. M	
3. G		11. O	
4. D		12. C	
5. E		13. B	
6. H		14. J	
7. L		15. N	
8. A			

Page 12

1. ache—dull pain; soreness
2. argue—disagree; quarrel
3. bulge—puff up; balloon
4. check—examine; inspect
5. earnest—serious; grave
6. flutter—flap; beat
7. hesitate—pause; delay
8. jealous—envious; covetous
9. locate—find; discover
10. murmur—whisper; mutter
11. object—thing/something; protest
12. perform—play; fulfill
13. prance—leap; spring; jump
14. scamper—run; dart
15. tilt—slant; slope

Page 13

1. A		11. H	
2. S		12. A	
3. A		13. S	
4. H		14. H	
5. S		15. H	
6. H		16. A	
7. H		17. S	
8. S		18. H	
9. A		19. S	
10. S		20. A	

Answer Key (cont.

Page 14
1. bor'-row
2. at'-tic
3. ban'-ner
4. bliz'-zard
5. ef-fect'
6. flut'-ter
7. hob'-by
8. let'-tuce
9. mit'-ten
10. stal'-lion
11. soc'-cer
12. pat'-tern
13. stub'-born
14. puz'-zle
15. lad'-der
16. fal'-ling
17. but'-ter

Page 15
1. a'-ble
2. bat'-tle
3. cas'-tle
4. cou'-ple
5. grum'-ble
6. jin'-gle
7. mum'-ble
8. pad'-dle
9. stum'-ble
10. tan'-gle
11. ta'-ble
12. no'-ble
13. sin'-gle
14. dou'-ble
15. tri'-ple
16. noo'-dle
17. tur'-tle

Page 16
1. ar'-tist
2. as-tound'
3. bam-boo'
4. car'-go
5. dis'-ease
6. ex'-plore
7. mix'-ture
8. sus'-pect
9. win'-ter
10. van'-ish

11. mes'-sage
12. lis'-ten
13. pon'-der
14. an'-swer
15. stum'-ble
16. ug'-ly
17. trum'-pet

Page 17
1. bi'-cy-cle
2. bi'-na-ry
3. cu'-ri-ous
4. de'-gree
5. fa'-vor-ite
6. hu'-man
7. mo'-tion
8. po'-lar
9. de'-serve
10. ze'-ro
11. pa'-per
12. ca'-ble
13. No'-vem-ber
14. jo'-ker
15. re'-ceive
16. cu'-cum-ber
17. ti'-ger

Page 18
1. a-corn, #4
2. at-ten-tion, #1 and #3
3. cob-bler, #1 and #3
4. De-cem-ber, #4
5. cor-ral, #1
6. bee-tle, #2 and #4
7. bot-tle, #1, #2, and #3
8. dan-dy, #3
9. blub-ber, #1 and #3
10. Oc-to-ber, #3
11. min-strel, #3
12. sto-len, #4
13. sta-ble, #2 and #4
14. van-ish, #3
15. trop-i-cal, #3

Page 19
1. cars
2. desks
3. houses
4. trees

5. boys
6. boxes
7. churches
8. dishes
9. dresses
10. quartzes
11. sketches
12. lenses
13. taxes
14. businesses
15. glasses

Page 20
1. babies
2. donkeys
3. guys
4. countries
5. copies
6. ladies
7. days
8. berries
9. valleys
10. policies
11. attorneys
12. delays
13. centuries
14. flies
15. bunnies

Page 21
1. children
2. feet
3. geese
4. men
5. mice
6. oxen
7. teeth
8. women
9. deer
10. fish
11. moose
12. sheep

Page 22
1. illogical = il + logical = not having logic
2. illegal = il + legal = not legal
3. impatient = im + patient = not having patience

4. inactive = in + active = not active
5. inattentive = in + attentive = not paying attention
6. incomplete = in + complete = not complete
7. indirect = in + direct = not direct
8. inhuman = in + human = not human
9. irregular = ir + regular = not regular
10. nonsense = non + sense = not making sense
11. nonstop = non + stop = not stopping
12. unpleasant = un + pleasant = not pleasant
13. unnatural = un + natural = not natural
14. unnecessary = un + necessary = not necessary

Page 23
1. C or G
2. B
3. F
4. D
5. C or G
6. A
7. E
8. untangle
9. reproduce
10. precaution
11. mislead
12. incomplete
13. biannual
14. tricycle

Page 24
1. actor—one who acts
2. childless—one who does not have children
   childish—one who acts like a child
3. thankful—grateful or full of thanks
   thankless—without gratitude
4. collectable;

Answer Key *(cont.)*

collectible—worthy to collect.

5. meanest—most mean

6. changeable—having the ability to change

7. Haitian—a person from the country of Haiti

Page 27

Page 31

1. equator: an imaginary line that divides Earth into hemispheres

2. geography: the study of the earth's physical features, its people, resources, and climate

3. hemisphere: one half of a sphere (e.g., Earth)

4. key: a list or chart that explains map symbols

5. latitude: the position of a place, measured in degrees north or south of the equator. These lines run east to west.

6. legend: the words written beneath or beside a map or chart that explains it

7. longitude: the position of a place, measured in degrees east or west of the prime meridian

8. meridians: imaginary circles around the earth's surface

9. polar: to do with or near the icy regions around the North or South Pole

10. prime meridian: the meridian that divides the earth into its hemispheres.

11. rural: to do with the countryside or farming

12. scale: the ratio between the measurements on a map or model and the actual measurements

13. symbol: a design or object that represents something else

14. tropics: the hot area of the earth near the equator

15. urban: to do with the city or living in the city

Page 32

1. B
2. A
3. F
4. G
5. D
6. E
7. C

Page 33

1. lbs.
2. oz.
3. >
4. m
5. in., ft.

Page 34

1. I.
2. E.
3. B.
4. G.
5. C.
6. F.
7. A.
8. H.
9. J.
10. D.

Page 35

1. Number sentences must be addition.

2. Number sentences must be multiplication.

3. Number sentences must be division.

4. Number sentences must be subtraction.

5. S + S+ S, *or* side + side + side

6. 12 square units

7. C

8. _____

9. X

10. $3 + 6 = 9$ *or* $6 + 3 = 9$, 6 *or* $9 - 6 = 3$ *or* $9 - 3$

Page 36

1. experiment
2. hypothesis
3. observe
4. analyze
5. data
6. cite
7. chart
8. variable

Answer to the Riddle: evidence

Page 37

1. bird
2. racket
3. poem
4. tall (or long)
5. Abraham
6. nut
7. soft
8. sand
9. window
10. read
11. teeth
12. Snow
13. cut
14. sock *or* shoe
15. hands

Page 38

1. Bob, Otto
2. did
3. civic
4. noon
5. nun
6. ewe
7. mum
8. peep
9. Tut
10. kayak
11. tot
12. Anna, Hannah
13. level
14. gag
15. solos

Page 39

Page 40

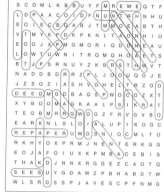

2. a
3. b
4. d
5. b
7. d
8. a
9. d

Page 43

10. a
11. c
12. d
13. b
14. b
15. a
16. d
17. c
18. b
19. c

Page 44

20. a
21. c
22. b
23. b
24. c
25. c
26. d
27. d

Page 45

28. b
29. a
30. c
31. a
32. d
33. b
34. c
35. a
36. a